Unfinished & Uncollected

Other publications by George Economou

POETRY
The Georgics
Landed Natures
Poems for Self-Therapy
Ameriki; Book One and Selected Earlier Poems
Voluntaries
harmonies & fits
Century Dead Center
Ananios of Kleitor *

TRANSLATIONS
Philodemos, His Twenty-Nine Extant Poems
William Langland's Piers Plowman, A Verse Translation of the C Version
I've Gazed So Much, Poems by C.P. Cavafy
Acts of Love, Ancient Greek Poetry from Aphrodite's Garden
Half an Hour, Poems by C. P. Cavafy
Complete Plus — The Poems of C.P. Cavafy in English *

CRITICISM
The Goddess Natura in Medieval Literature
Janus Witness: Testament of a Greek American Poet

EDITOR
Geoffrey Chaucer, A Collection of Original Articles
In Pursuit of Perfection: Courtly Love in Medieval Literature, with Joan M. Ferrante
Proensa, An Anthology of Troubadour Poetry Translated by Paul Blackburn
Poem of the Cid, translated by Paul Blackburn

(* indicates a Shearsman title)

Unfinished & Uncollected

Finishing Cavafy's Unfinished Poems

followed by

Uncollected Poems & Translations

George Economou

Shearsman Books

First published in the United Kingdom in 2015 by
Shearsman Books
50 Westons Hill Drive
Emersons Green
BRISTOL
BS16 7DF

Shearsman Books Ltd Registered Office
30–31 St. James Place, Mangotsfield, Bristol BS16 9JB
(this address not for correspondence)

www.shearsman.com

ISBN 978-1-84861-436-9

Copyright © George Economou, 2015.

The right of George Economou to be identified as the author and translator of this work has been asserted by him in accordance with the Copyrights, Designs and Patents Act of 1988.
All rights reserved.

Acknowledgements

Grateful acknowledgement is made to the following journals, internet sites, and anthologies in which many of the poems and translations published here previously appeared:
American Poetry Review, Asymptote, Contact 2, Golden Handcuffs Review, Jacket2, New Letters, Nomadics, PN Review, Poems and Poetics, Poeticanet, Pomegranate Seeds, Sulfur, The Café Review, The Charioteer, The Iowa Review, The Left-Hand Sideshow, and *Truck.*

Thanks to Andrea Augé for the author photo on the back cover.

Contents

All-American	9
FINISHING CAVAFY'S UNFINISHED POEMS	11
The Newspaper Story	13
It Must Have Been the Drinks	14
And Above All Cynegirus	15
Antiochus Cyzicenus	16
On the Pier	17
Athanasius	18
The Bishop Pegasius	19
After the Swim	20
Birth of a Poem	21
Ptolemy Benefactor (or Malefactor)	22
The Dynasty	23
From the "Off the Record" History	24
Julian's Rescue	26
The Photograph	27
The Saintly Seven Children	28
Around the Colonnaded Groves	29
The Patriarch	30
On Epiphany	31
Epitaph of a Samian	32
Prick of Conscience	33
The Emperor Conon	34
Hunc Deorum Templa	35
Crime	36
Of the Sixth or Seventh Century	37
Tigranokerta	38
Being Left	39
Nothing About the Lacedaimonians	40
Zenobia *First Version*	41
Zenobia *Second Version*	42
Foursome	43
Agelaos	44
Diverse Sketches	45
Notes	48
Dates of Cavafy's Unfinished Poems	56

Uncollected Poems & Translations

Poems
"Kassandra's Story"	61
The Amorous Drift of the First Hoplite on the Right Wing	63
Day of Disembarkation	64
The Birth of Stand-Up	65
Débat de l'âme et du corps	67
Elegiac	69
Apotropaic	71
The Irrepressible Residue at the Bottom of the Pensioner's Heart	72
A Five in One Wedding Song	73
The Twa Poets in Brooklyn Heights	75
Narcissus Sestina	78
Pantoum for C.P. Cavafy and a Translator	80
Who Wants Ice Cream?	81
The Girl in the Gown	82
Fuck Your Votive Light	83
Five by Georgios Arkadios	84
Montana 1939–	87

Translations
Archilochos	Rough Trade	97
Anacreon	"Once he stepped out wearing outlandish…"	98
Sappho	"It is for you, those lovely gifts…"	99
	The Brothers Poem	100
C. P. Cavafy	Second Odyssey	101
	The End of Antony	103
	And I Leaned and Lay on Their Beds	104
Michalis Katsaros	Those You See	105
Luis Cortest	The Subway Station	106

For Rochelle,
Always and All Ways

All-American

The Unexamined Ethnic Life
Is Not Worth Living.

Finishing Cavafy's Unfinished

> "It could well be that there is no really felicitous solution to the editorial challenges these texts present to the would-be translator."
> —Karen Emmerich, "'Impossible Things': Editing and Translating C.P. Cavafy's Unfinished Poems,"
> *Arion* 17.3 (Winter, 2010), 122.

The following poems, based on diverse drafts and sketches preserved in the Cavafy archive and published along with proposed reconstructions in the superb collection entitled *ATELI PIIMATA* (Unfinished Poems) edited by Professor Renata Lavagnini of the University of Palermo (Athens: Ikaros Press, 1994), present as poetry in English versions of poems that have not been fully realized in their original Greek. In my effort to render them as poems in English, I have relied upon an approach of trans-composition, which combines the work of translator and poet in a collaborative process with Cavafy that I have previously described as *un métissage de l'écriture*. The balance between these two kinds of work within the approach to each poem necessarily differs according to the textual complexity of each of Cavafy's unfinished poems. The more drafts, variants, and marginal comments and corrections in the condition of an original, the greater the possibilities the poet's work will play a major role in the refashioning of its elements into a finished poem in English. In all of my versions, however, I have felt free to follow a poet's instinct rather than the conventional demands of a translator's craft. Though I make no claim they represent how Cavafy would have finished his preliminary or ongoing workings of them, I will insist that they remain true rather than traitorous to the poetic potential inherent in their unfinished states.

George Economou

The Newspaper Story

Dejected, reading the newspaper while riding the tram:
he came across an apparent crime in the Police Blotter,
a crime that had taken place the night before
between ten and eleven. The murderer had not yet been found.
The newspaper story, quite justly,
abhorred the murder, but righteously
showed its utter contempt
for the victim's degenerate way of life,
for that individual's depravity.

He read all about it, the contempt… and grieving in silence,
remembered an evening between ten and midnight a year ago
they had spent together in a room
(the only time—barely knowing each other by sight)
in a half-hotel, half brothel. Never—not even
in the street—did they ever meet again.
It described the wound in detail
and surmised blackmail must have had something to do with it.
The contempt…and he, grieving in silence,
remembered the sweet lips and the white, exceptional
sublime flesh he hadn't kissed enough.

Dejected, he read the story in the newspaper.

The body was discovered at about eleven at night
near the docks. It was not definite after all
that a crime had been committed,
a slight chance it was an accident, wasn't intentional.
The newspaper expressed some pity, but righteously
showed its indignation and contempt
for the victim's degenerate way of life.

It Must Have Been the Drinks

The house is closed and nobody's coming,
it's about ten and you'll reappear
the way you were, the way you are, unchanged.
Avoid the mirror—remember, as you were and still are.

Must have been my drinking in the evening,
must have been my nodding off, I'd been tired all day.

The black wooden column's fading away,
with its archaic capital, and the dining room door,
the red arm-chair and the small divan.
A street in Marseille's coming in their place,
and my set-free, unshrinking soul,
relieved of the weight of years,
reappears and moves there,
with the form of a sensitive, sensuous youth—
a dissolute youth: let us say this as well.

Must have been my drinking in the evening,
must have been my nodding off, I'd been so tired all day.

I can't imagine him still alive and old.
No matter what life's done to him,
in the poem he remains as he was
when I knew him in that back street
in Marseille one blissful night,
in the frame of a happy, dissolute youth,
where he knows no shame, no, not he for sure.

And Above All Cynegirus

Being from a prominent Italian family
and in his early twenties,
in the custom of the wide world of Greek culture,
he came to Smyrna to learn all about rhetoric
and to become proficient in its discourse.

So today he hears, without paying
the least attention to him, the famous sophist
who talks about Athens, who gesticulates
and, loaded with enthusiasm, does the story
of Miltiades and the glorious battle of Marathon.
He thinks about tonight's drinking party
and his imagination conjures up a tender face,
beguiling lips he can't wait to kiss....
He thinks about the good time he's having here.
But his money's running out, and in a few months
he'll return to Rome. And he remembers
the debts he's piled up there. That he must go back
to the dreadful rut of playing the deadbeat,
of scrounging up the means to live as he deserves
(he *is* from a prominent Italian house).
Now for the will of old man Fulvius,
ah, if he could only see it. Just know
how much he's getting from that dirty old man
(two, three years, how long can he last!).
Will he leave him half, a third? True enough,
he's already bailed him out of debt twice.

The sophist overcome with emotion,
on the verge of tears, tells about Cynegirus.

Antiochus Cyzicenus

The people of Syria tolerate him:
just as long as nobody stronger turns up.
And what "Syria"? It's almost half-gone,
with its mini-kingdoms, with John Hyrcanus' invasions,
with the cities that have declared independence.

From the time the country began, historians say,
 it stretched from the Aegean all the way to India.
From the Aegean all the way to India! But hold on.
Let's take a look at these puppets
and the animals he has brought us.

On the Pier

An intoxicating night, in the dark, on the pier,
then later in the tiny room of a hotel
of ill-repute—where we surrendered completely to
our sick and lovely passion, hour upon hour to our kind of love—
until the new day lit up on the window-panes.

The face of night this evening, just like another,
returns me to a night from the distant past.

Moonless, pitch-dark
(as was fitting). Our assignation
on the pier, so very far away
from the park, the cafés and the bars.

Athanasius

Aboard a boat on the wide Nile,
with two trustworthy monks for companions,
the fugitive and tormented Athanasius
—the righteous, the pious, keeper of the true faith—
was praying. Hounded by enemies,
there was little hope of deliverance.
Into the strong headwind,
their flimsy boat could barely make its way.

When he finished his prayer,
he turned his distressed gaze
upon his companions— and was amazed
to see their peculiar smiles.
While he was praying, the monks
had discerned what was going on
in Mesopotamia, the monks
were aware that at that moment
that piece of dirt Julian had expired,
that the depraved Apostate lived no more.

The Bishop Pegasius

They stepped into the splendid temple of Athena
the "Christian" bishop Pegasius
the royal "Christian" young prince Julian.
They looked with tender yearning at the statues—
but their conversation was hesitant,
full of insinuations and ambiguities,
suspicious and precautionary phrasings,
for they were not at all sure of each other,
and consequently afraid of being outed,
the fake Christian bishop Pegasius
the royal fake Christian young Julian.

After the Swim

Both naked when they stepped out of the sea on the Samian shore
after their refreshing swim—
a burning hot summer's day—
they took their time dressing, unhappy to cover up
with their gold-embroidered silk threads
their beautiful lithesome nakedness
that so perfectly accorded with their handsome faces.

Ah, how refined the ancient Greeks were
to depict youth's loveliness
utterly naked.

He wasn't so far off the mark, their teacher, old Gemistus
(let Lord Andronicus and the patriarch suspect him all they like)
to want and exhort us to revert to paganism.
My sacred faith always unshakably reverent—
but Gemistus still makes sense up to a point.

A big influence on the youth back then
had the teachings of Georgius Gemistus,
who was most wise and so very eloquent,
Hellenic education's messenger.

Birth of a Poem

One night when the lovely moonlight
streamed into my room… imagination,
taking hold of something from life: a very small thing—
a distant scene, a distant pleasure—
brought its own vision of a body,
its own vision to a bed made for love…

Ptolemy Benefactor (or Malefactor)

The poet—of definitely limited worldly renown,
though in the palace a pleasing regular—
was performing at length for King Ptolemy
passages from his poem regarding the reactions
the campaign of Agesilaus might have sparked in Greece.

At the peak of his corpulence and indolence
and drowsy from overeating, Ptolemy,
aka Fatso or The Bladder, observed,
"Learned poet, your well-made verses are somewhat
over the top, and your remarks about Greek history,
about which we know a little ourselves, lame and slippery."
"Glorious Ptolemy, these are minor issues."

"How minor issues? You express yourself explicitly,
*'The Greeks' exalted pride… the roused up
unadulterated patriotism… the uncurbed charge
towards heroism of the Greeks quite apparent'.*"

"Glorious Ptolemy, these Greeks
are Greeks belonging to Art, poetic types
obliged to feel as I determine."

Scandalized, Ptolemy muttered an objection,
"The Alexandrians are incurably flimsy."

The poet: "Glorious Ptolemy,
among Alexandrians you are Number One."

"Up to a point," retorted Ptolemy, "up to a point.
I am of pure as pure can be Macedonian birth.—
Ah, what a great nation Macedonia, the max,
learned poet, brimful with daring and wisdom."

And heavy as a stone owing to his massive flesh
and somnolent from his overeating,
this purest of the pure Macedonian
could barely keep his eyes open.

The Dynasty

Potbelly's boys: Chickpea, banished
in disgrace from Alexandria, makes for Cyprus.
And Interloper, directly quitting Cyprus,
grabs hold of Alexandria. All this nasty work
mapped out by the malign Scarlet Snatch.
The bantering swift-witted Alexandrians
sure knew how to name them well. Better matched
with "Interloper," "Potbelly," "Chickpea," and "Scarlet Snatch"
than *Ptolemy*, than *Cleopatra*.

From the "Off the Record" History

Often the expression on Justinian's face
produced terror and abhorrence in his attendants.
They dared not speak of what they suspected,
until one night by chance they ascertained
that he was a demon straight out of Hell:
late at night he came out of his apartment and roamed
through the palace chambers and halls headless.

Julian's Rescue

When the berserk soldiers killed
the relatives of the deceased Constantine,
and at the end endangered through their harrowing
frenzy even the little boy—a six-year old—
of Caesar Julius Constantius,
some Christian priests, full of compassion,
horror and indignation, took possession
of him and set him into the asylum
of the church. There they rescued him, the six-year old Julian.

Yet it's necessary for us to say
this information's source is Christian.
But it's by no means unlikely to be true.
Nothing about it appears to be
historically uncommon: Christ's priests
coming to the rescue of an innocent Christian child.

And if true—mightn't it be that the so very philosophical
Augustus elucidated this as well, recalling
his early days in his oration to the sun-god Helios,
"but into Lethe may that darkness fall"?

The Photograph

Looking at the photograph of one of his partners,
his handsome—no, beautiful face
(lost for good now—dating back to
'Ninety-two, the thirty-year old picture),
the sadness of how brief it is overcame him.
But there is some consolation at least
in that he didn't—they didn't allow a single bit of stupid shame
to obstruct, to taint or distort their love.
To the idiots' jeers, "degenerates," "queers,"
their sense of eros paid no mind ever.

The Saintly Seven Children

How beautifully the *Synaxarion* puts it:
"Even as the king communed" with the saints
"and with the Bishops and many another nobleman,
the saints started to feel a little drowsy"
and delivered their souls unto God.

The Saintly Seven Children of Ephesus
who fled into a cave to hide out
from the Pagans' persecution, and there fell asleep;
and awoke the next morning. Next morning for them.
But in the interim two centuries had gone by.

One of them, Iamblichus, awoke the next morning
and went out to buy bread,
and was confronted with a new and different Ephesus,
sanctified throughout with churches and crosses.

And the Saintly Seven Children were overjoyed,
and the Christians honored and venerated them;
and even the king came from Constantinople,
Theodosius, the son of Arcadius,
and that most devout of men, as was due, venerated them as well.

And the Saintly Seven Children were rejoicing
in that lovely world, that Christian one,
that sanctified with churches and crosses one.

But now look how everything was so different
and they had so much to learn and to say
(and also such mighty joy can itself be fatiguing)
that the Saintly Seven Children were soon tired out,
having come from another world, from almost two centuries ago,
and nodding off during the conversation—
they closed their saintly eyes.

Around the Colonnaded Groves

—*Apollonius of Tyana seeing from Ephesus
what's happening in Rome*

Domitian had gone out-of-his-mind mad,
because of him the provinces were suffering terribly.
In Ephesus, as elsewhere, much despair.
When out of the blue, one day Apollonius was speaking
around the colonnaded groves where the statues are,
he suddenly seemed distracted
and to be giving his talk as if in a trance.
Right then he stopped talking and called out
that "*smite the tyrant*" in the midst
of his large and completely astonished audience.
In that moment of detachment his soul saw
Stephanus, in Rome, striking Domitian
with his sword, who trying to defend himself
with a golden goblet had thrown Stephanus down,
beating him doggedly, and finally the pack
of spearmen entering and directly
finishing off the base (almost unconscious) king.

The Patriarch

That insolent ingrate John,
who owed his being patriarch
to the kind regard
of Lord John Cantacuzenus
(best of men among our people then,
wise, tolerant, patriotic, brave and able),
put on airs of wisdom, that patriarch
without principle, and said he'd see to it
that the hundred year old injustice done to John Lascaris
would not be repeated (not understanding,
the lame-brain, what a great insult
his words were to the start of the Palaeologue reign).
He knew for sure, that miserable excuse
for a human being, that there was no danger at all
to Lord Andronicus' nine year old boy
from the honorable, loyal, and selfless
Lord John Cantacuzenus,
no danger to the life or accession of John Palaeologos.
That miserable obscenity knew, yet still tried
in every way to play the demagogue.

On Epiphany

When on Epiphany they arranged to repeat
the same stunt they had pulled on Christmas Day,
when they brought back their gang of thugs
aiming to use the boy to work up
the people once again (the poor kid John,
the good Lord Andronicus' son and heir,
who should have been in her and her son's care,

when at Epiphany they arranged to repeat
the rabble's vile and vulgar insults
and the disgusting insinuendoes about her,
she couldn't take the agony a second time
and in that squalid room that served as her prison cell
the Lady Cantacuzene gave up her soul.

The Lady Cantacuzene's end, come so piteously,
I've culled from Nicephoros Gregoras' History.
In the historical work of the emperor
John Cantacuzenus it's portrayed rather
differently, yet no less grievously.

Epitaph of a Samian

—The following is one of the poems, referring to times before the Persian Wars, that Kleonymos, son of Timandros, wrote in Seleucia, a poet patronized by King Antiochos Epiphanes.

Stranger, here by the Ganges lies a man
from Samos. A life full of pain, heartaches,
and toil I lived in this barbarous land.
This grave scooped beside the river partakes
of many woes. A consuming passion
for gold spurred me into a hateful trade.
Shipwrecked by storms on the Indian Ocean,
I was sold as a slave. Up in age, made
a worn out old thing, worked to my last gasp—
for forty years no Greek I spoke or heard.
So now I escape my brute sorrow's grasp,
and descend to Hades with grief deterred.
   Here then with family and friends I'll speak
   in the hereafter in excellent Greek.

Prick of Conscience

Tell this remorse of yours to ease up,
certainly a virtue, but dangerously one-sided.
Don't be so fixed on the past or oppress yourself so much.
Don't take yourself so seriously.
The harm you caused was smaller
than you suppose, much smaller.
The quality that stirs this remorse now
lay hidden deep inside you even then.
Look at how an incident that out of the blue
surfaces in your memory explains
the motive for an act that seemed at the time
without merit, but is quite justifiable now.
Don't trust in your memory so utterly;
you've forgotten a lot—all kinds of stuff—
that would have sufficed to justify you.

And don't suppose you knew the injured party
that well. He must have had gifts you didn't know about;
nor perhaps were those scratches the ones
you suppose (being ignorant about his life)
were the terrible wounds you inflicted on him.

Don't trust that feeble memory of yours.
Soften this bite of inwit, which again and again
bares a sort of specious bias against you.

The Emperor Conon

Hey virtuous patriarch, hey righteous patriarch,
don't con yourself into believing it's impossible
for the demolition of the holy icons to happen
just because the emperor Conon hasn't shown up yet.

Hey unlucky patriarch, no-no don't con yourself:
abysmal Leo, look here, just stepped into your chamber
and means to slip you his baptismal name.

Hunc Deorum Templa*

Blind old woman, were you a hidden pagan?
Or a Christian? Your turned out to be true
message—that he who entered
Vienne so lionized, the glorious
Caesar Julian, was predisposed
to serve the temples of the (false) gods—
your turned out to be true message,
blind old woman, did you speak it, as was meet, with sadness
as I'd like to surmise, or, you hideous wretch! with delight?

* *For the record, Cavafy gave the title "Hunc Deorum Templis" to his drafts of this poem, having incorrectly copied the word* templa *from the account in the blind old woman's outcry,* exclamavit hunc deorum templa reparaturum, *in his fourth-century A.D. Latin source, Ammianus Marcellinus, XV, 8, 22.*

Crime

*This was found among some poet's papers.
It's dated, but quite illegibly.
A one scarcely visible, next nine, next
one, the fourth number looks like a nine.*

Stavros dealt out our shares in the loot.
The alpha youth in our gang,
smart, tough, and too beautiful for words.
The most capable, though except for me
(I was twenty) he was the youngest.
My guess is he wasn't quite twenty-three.

Our haul was three thousand pounds.
He kept, as we convinced him was fair, half of it.

But now, at eleven at night, we were working on
putting him on the lam the next morning,
before the police found out about the burglary.
Not a lightweight heist, but grand larceny.

We were down in a cellar, safe-housed in a basement.
After we'd decided on the plan for his escape,
the other three left us, me and Stavros,
with the understanding they'd return at five.

There was a ripped up mattress on the floor.
Dead-tired, the two of us dropped. And with our shaky
feelings, and the extreme fatigue,
and with the anguish over his getaway
in the morning—I hardly realized, didn't realize at all
that in these last hours together our love had come to its end.

Of the Sixth or Seventh Century

Let's go back in our beloved city's story
to that very interesting and moving
Alexandria of the sixth century, or the early seventh
before the advent of the mighty Arab offensive.
She still speaks Greek, officially at least;
maybe not so trippingly on the tongue, though respectably,
she still speaks our language.
One day it will die out of the Greek destiny,
but for now it's still hanging on as much as it can.

It isn't unnatural for us to concentrate so
emotionally on this specific period of hers,
we, even a poet like me, who now revive
the sound of Greek in her soil.

Tigranokerta

I owe a debt of gratitude, I'll admit,
to my compatriot and relative
(says she's my supposed father's sister)
the aged madam Kerkó, who invited me here
to this newborn city Tigranokerta
the most prosperous, the most fortunate.

The theater's one way I can get some attention:
I do tolerably well as an actor. This here
is no Alexandria, and it's not an Athens.
I played a not too bad Sophoclean Haimon
and a so-so Euripidean Hippolytos as well.
The audiences said that their city
had never seen a more attractive actor—or young man.
A couple of rich citizens, marvelously extravagant,
took a special interest in me.
The kind of thing Kerkó the expert attends to
(even skimming half for her go-between job, the low-down thief).
Ah, what an exceptional place this Tigranokerta!—
as long as it lasts, that is, because it's a sure thing
the Romans will destroy it in the end.
King Tigranes is a dreamer.
But that's nothing to me. At the most
I'll stick around a few months—and after that split.

And then I could care less if the Romans waste
Tigranokerta and Kerkó with it.

Being Left

He was much too sophisticated and much too smart,
a young man from the top of high society,
to take it, as if he'd been the butt of a joke,
like some kind of tragedy, being left that way.
Besides, when his friend told him, "Our love
is forever"—both he who spoke it
and he who heard it understood this for the convention it is.
After a movie and then ten minutes
of hard drinking in the bar one night
their desire lit up their eyes and blood
and they left together and that "forever" was uttered.

That "forever," anyway, held out for three years.
It seldom ever lasts that long.

He was much too sophisticated and much too smart
to consider this thing tragic
and much too beautiful—with his face and physique—
for it to affect in the least his natural vanity.

Nothing About the Lacedaimonians

Love sincerity, sure
and serve it.
But with moderation, knowing it's quite likely
you will come to a point where sincerity doesn't work.
It is good, and what a wonderful feeling.
You'll express yourself with honor and sincerity
about many things and you will be helpful.
They will justly hold you in esteem: what a forthright, sincere man!
But mix your wine with water: don't be so cocksure of yourself
because (as you know) "Nothing about the Lacedaimonians."

Zenobia

First Version

Now that Zenobia's become queen of numerous great lands,
now that she's the wonder of the Anatolian world,
and now that even the Romans fear her,
why shouldn't her greatness be fulfilled?
Why should she be pigeonholed as Woman/ Asian?

Two scholars well versed in history
will prepare her genealogy forthwith.

Look at how she's clearly descended from the Lagids.
Look at how clearly from Macedonia + +

[According to Lavagnini's editorial apparatus, each of the two crosses after the word "Macedonia" represents approximately two illegible letters in Cavafy's one-sheet manuscript. The rest is silence.]

Zenobia

Second Version

Now that Zenobia's become queen of numerous great lands,
now that she's the wonder of the Anatolian world,
and now that even the Romans fear her,
why shouldn't her greatness be fulfilled?
Why should she be pigeonholed as Woman/ Asian?

Two scholars well versed in history
will prepare her genealogy forthwith.

Look at how she's clearly descended from the Lagids.
Look at how clearly from Macedonia *her bloodline flows
into the stream of her noble Semitic spring: "Augusta" suits her well.*

Clearly one day now she'll parade through Rome in wraps of gold.

Foursome

Their way of making money   was surely not aboveboard.
But they're street-smart boys,   the four of them, who've figured out
how to do their business   steering clear of the police.
Apart from being smart,   they're super tough together.
Since two of them are joined   by the bond of pleasure
so are the other two joined   by the bond of pleasure.
They can dress to kill   as is quite suitable
for such handsome boys,   and the theater and bars,
and their snazzy car,   and a trip now and then
to Cairo in the winter,   they are missing nothing.

Their way of making money   was surely not aboveboard,
with an occasional scare   of getting cut up
or of doing time in jail.   But look at how Love
has such power to take   the dirty money they make
and fashion it anew   into something blindingly pure.

That money none of them   wants for himself or
for personal interests.   None of them tallies it up
grossly or with greed.   They never take note
if one brings in less   or another more.
In common they hold   their money, using it
to dress with style,   to bankroll the outlay
that makes their lives   elegant and well-suited
to such handsome boys,   for helping out their friends,
and then, as is their way,   just forget about it.

Agelaos

To the assembly at Naupactus Agelaos
told it like it is. Stop fighting each other,
Greek against Greek. The conflict that menaces
us is happening nearby right now. Either Carthage
or Rome will win and then head for us. Oh, King
Philip, regard all Greeks as your own.
If it's wars you want, get ready
to confront Italy's winner.
This is no time to be fighting each other.
Oh, King Philip, save Greece.

Wise words, but they didn't sink in.
In those frightful, accursed days
of battle at Cynocephalae, Magnesia, and Pydna,
many a Greek would remember them well,
those wise words that didn't sink in.

Diverse Sketches

A son of a slave slave, bereft of hope and joy,
stooped over the same chore for forty years
at his workbench aligns the new coins
to be issued by the people of Nicaea.
One by one he picks them up and measures;
and with eyes clouded by age, he meticulously
checks whether the inscription is right.
If he screws up again, he'll pay dearly, they said,
and with his hands shaking, here he goes:
"*Under the rule of Serverus the world prospers.*"

*

The reds, the yellows, and the blues
are beautiful in flowers, I confess.
But for color as I imagine it,
color constant and pure,
my mind doesn't turn to flowers but
to the red of rubies and coral,
to the yellow of topaz and gold,
and of sapphires and turquoise the blue.

*

*When I kissed Agathon, my soul rose to my lips,
in hopes, poor thing, of making the great leap across.*
Plato, *The Greek Anthology*, 5.78

There was nothing in the least romantic
about the way he told me, "Maybe I'm going to die."
He meant it as a joke, the kind of crack
a twenty-three year old boy would make.
As for me—at twenty-five—I didn't take it seriously.
Not at all (luckily) like the pseudo-sentimental poetry

that tugs at the heart-strings of fancy (ridiculous) ladies
who sigh away over nothing.

And yet when I found myself
outside the door of his house
it dawned on me this wasn't a joking matter.
It was quite possible he was dying. And fearfully so
I dashed up the three flights of stairs,
and without exchanging a single word,
kissed his brow, kissed his eyes, kissed his mouth,
his chest, his hands, kissed his every limb and beauty
so that it seemed—just as the divine lines
of Plato say—that my soul rose up to my lips.

I was too sick to attend the funeral.
All alone over his white coffin
his mother mourned him purely.

*

Fifteen years after Julian's death
and into the first of Theodosius' rule:
in the great hall of his father's mansion
a young Alexandrian awaited
the visit of a beloved friend.

In order to pass the time more easily
he picked up and browsed in the nearest book.

It was by that nasty-tempered sophist Libanius
who, meaning to put down the Christians,
cited Julian's sentence in which he forbade
them from teaching the pagan poets and ordered
them to stick to their own Galilean scriptures.
"Yes, indeed," murmured the young Alexandrian,
"first Matthew, first Luke."

As for the rest, then, of Julian's froth
(bear in mind Theodosius would annul that decree of his),
"Homer and Hesiod," drew no more than a smile.

Notes

'And Above All Cynegirus' (p.15)
This poem's ironic title is a quote from one of the satires of Lucian of Samosata (120–c.180 A.D.), *Teacher of Orators*. The best-known account of the historical event gone stale in the hands of sophists like the one performing in Cavafy's poem is in *The Histories of Herodotus*, The Sixth Book, Entitled Erato, 114: "It was in the struggle here that Callimachus the polemarch, after greatly distinguishing himself, lost his life; Stesilaüs too, the son of Thrasilaüs, one of the generals was slain; and Cynaegirus, the son of Euphorion *[brother of Aeschylus]*, having seized on a vessel of the enemy's by the ornament at the stern, had his hand cut off by the blow of an axe, and so perished, as likewise did many other Athenians of note and name." (Translation by George Rawlinson)

'Antiochus Cyzicenus' (p.16)
Antiochus IX Cyzicenus (c. 137–96 B.C.) and his half-brother Antiochus VIII Grypus (Hook Nose) ruled, mostly on unfriendly terms, separate parts of the Seleucid Empire during a period of tumultuous civil strife and disintegration. John Hyrcanus (c. 175–104 B.C.), a High Priest and son of Simon Maccabee, took advantage of this Syrian instability by leading military campaigns to recover and increase Judean territories. Antiochus Cyzicenus was infamous for his drunkeness and excessive life-style, which included an inordinate fondness for mimes, puppetry, all manner of performance crafts, and hunting wild animals.

'Athanasius' (p.18)
Bishop of Alexandria and one of the most revered Doctors of the early church, Athanasius (c. 296–373 A.D.) was known as the "Father of Orthodoxy," especially for his powerful and effective opposition to the Arian heresy. The subject of this poem is based on a story about his problems later in his life with Julian, Roman Emperor (361–363 A.D.), originally a Christian who renounced his religion and converted to paganism, earning the epithet "the Apostate." The closing lines of this poem refer to Julian's death in battle on June 26, 363. That this and four other works about Julian, 'The Bishop Pegasius,' 'Julian's Rescue,' 'Hunc Templa Deorum,' and the fourth and last of 'Diverse Sketches,' appear among Cavafy's 'Unfinished Poems' should come as no surprise to readers familiar with his collected poems, among which there are several more that he wrote over the course of his career.

'The Bishop Pegasius' (p.19)
In 362 A.D., a year before his death, the Emperor Julian wrote a letter in defense of a former Christian bishop, Pegasius, whose standing as a pagan had been seriously questioned. Julian refers to a visit he made to the city of Ilion in Asia

Minor in 355, during which he was given a tour of the ancient temples by the then Bishop Pegasius. Having never met before, the two young men, both of them crypto-pagans and unsure of each other's belief, conversed in highly guarded language, according to Julian's account.

'After the Swim' (p.20)
Georgius Gemistus Plethon (c. 1355–c. 1452) was the preeminent Neoplatonist of Byzantium and the Western World of his time, who, near the end of his life, openly advocated belief in the ancient gods. Andronicus (d. 1429) was the son of the Emperor Manuel II Palaeologus, who reigned from 1391 to 1425. The "patriarch" refers to Georgius Scholarius, an Aristotelian and rival of Gemistus, who, some years before he became Gennadius II, Patriarch of Constantinople, after the Ottomans conquered the city in 1453, urged the Emperor Manuel to exile his Platonist opponent because of his suspiciously heretical pagan leanings. It is thought that Andronicus may have helped carry out his father's order to do so. These seemingly roundabout historical details subtly reinforce the impression that the two young swimmers in the poem were in fact students of a living Gemistus.

'Ptolemy Benefactor (or Malefactor)' (p.22-23)
Though Ptolemy VIII (c. 182–116 B.C.), who ruled Egypt during two separate periods, displayed a marked, if somewhat flamboyant, interest in poetry and literary matters (he once commented on the flowers in Calypso's garden), his historical legacy stands in doubly ironic contradiction to activities such as the one described in Cavafy's poem. As noted by the editor and translator of the poems of Ananios of Kleitor, Ptolemy instituted policies upon his return to power in 145 that caused the flight of most of Alexandria's intellectuals and scholars out of the country. That such a luminary as Aristarchus of Samothrace, the great chief librarian of Alexandria and editor of Homer, "who died on the island of Cyprus that same year, and so many others who were part of the city's celebrated creative and intellectual tradition departed in 145, has been charged to the recognition that life under the physically and morally gross Ptolemy VIII would have been intolerable to individuals of such preeminence, not to mention how dangerous it would have been to remain in Egypt for those who had opposed him during the earlier period of his rule (170–163). Such imputations may be further supported by noting that Ptolemy VIII's official royal titles, Euergetes (Benefactor) and Tryphon (Magnificent) were popularly reversed through the wordplay the ancients called *prosonomasia* to Kakegertes (Malefactor) and Physcon (Potbelly or Fatso), respectively, the latter jesting title being by far the most commonly and longest held among his subjects and subsequently by historians, for the murderous and vengeful—it goes without saying, lustful--Ptolemy exhibited an inordinate fondness for gauzy garments, through which he flaunted his disgusting corpulence. So the return of Physcon to Memphis as Pharaoh in 145

49

(this second reign ended with his death in 116) precipitated a voluntary exodus of scholars and intellectuals, whose number swelled through his own decrees of expulsion against Jews and other undesirables. The fortuitous cultural expansion that resulted from this emigration of eminent Alexandrians throughout the Hellenistic world to the great benefit of its Roman conquerors would have been completely unexpected by the likes of Ptolemy VIII, whose lack of anticipation of which could only be matched by his indifference to its significance. Like the tiny balls of fire and sparks scattered by an exploding Roman candle, the departing literati inseminated the entire Mediterranean with new poetic light."

The subject of the palace poet's performance, the campaign in 396 of Agesilaus, the king of Sparta from 399 to 360 B.C., against the Persians in order to protect cities allied to Sparta, was controversial among Greeks, as were his policies to gain military dominance in Greece itself. His military operations against the Persians, however, have been viewed as having inspired Alexander the Great and his father, Philip of Macedon.

'The Dynasty' (p.24)
In choosing this title over 'The House of Potbelly,' which he had tried out in an early draft, Cavafy initialized the irony and contempt that pervades this work. The events so tersely reported focus on the manipulations and favoritism of Potbelly/ Ptolemy's widow Cleopatra III, his niece-stepdaughter-second wife. Her nickname, "Κόκκη," denotes the color scarlet but also means in slang what is identified in Liddell & Scott as *pudenda muliebria*. During 108–107 B.C., she connived against her first-born son, Ptolemy IX, aka "Chickpea," in favor of her second one, Ptolemy X, the "Interloper."

'From the "Off the Record" History' (p.25)
Cavafy's authorities for this horror scene were J. B. Bury, *A History of the Later Roman Emperors from the Death of Theodosius I to the Death of Justinian (395– 565)*, vol. 2 (London, 1923), pp. 423-24) and the *Anecdota* or *Secret History* by Procopius (500–560 A.D.), who was Justinian's principal historian, writing two major works about his achievements, *The Wars of Justinian* and *The Buildings of Justinian*. But after becoming at some point bitterly disillusioned with Justinian and Theodora, he began recording his secret history and exposé, a combination of shocking personal revelations and, at times, wild gossip, alleging the emperor's demonic patrlineage and labeling the imperial couple as "*anthropodaimones* "(xii, 14).

'Julian's Rescue' (p.26)
Caesar Julius Constantius, a victim of a violent assassination plot against the recently deceased Constantine the Great's male relatives by one of his three sons and direct heirs in 337 A.D., was the late emperor's half-brother and Julian's father. Julian's later callous and hypocritical rejection of his early Christian life,

and his rescue along with it, is a direct quotation from the beginning of his *Oration IV*.

'The Saintly Seven Children' (p.28)
The story of The Seven Sleepers of Ephesus, which Edward Gibbon distinguished as "a memorable fable" among "the insipid legends of ecclesiastical history" in his *The Decline and Fall of the Roman Empire* (vol. 1, chapter xxxiii) was widely disseminated for centuries throughout the Christian world. The historical timeline begins with the persecution of Christians by the Roman emperor Decius in 250 A.D. and ends during the reign of the Eastern emperor Theodosius II (408–450). Cavafy's version, as stated in the poem's opening lines, is drawn from the *Synaxarion*, the great Orthodox Christian collection and calendar of saints' lives and their feast days, which commemorates the first sleep of the Saintly Seven Children on August 4 and their second one on October 22.

'Around the Colonnaded Groves' (p.29)
Cavafy's primary source for this and the three poems in the collected poetry, 'If Dead Then,' 'But Wise Men Apprehend What Is Imminent,' and 'Apollonius of Tyana in Rhodes,' that he wrote about the Neopythagorean magus and sage was the long, encomiastic life of Apollonius (c. 3 B. C–97 A.D.) by the Athenian sophist Philostratus (c. 170–c. 240 A.D.). In the fourth book of the biography, Apollonius has returned to Ephesus from Rome where he had been tried by the emperor Domitian (51–96 A.D.) for conspiracy and practicing magic, charges that he roundly denied, and in the course of lecturing to a large audience falls silent during an apparent moment of clairvoyance in which he sees and reports the assassination in Rome of the tyrannical emperor led by Stephanus, the empress Domitia's freedman servant.

'The Patriarch' and 'On Epiphany' (pp.30-31)
Having been appointed regent in 1341 A.D. upon the death of Byzantine Emperor Andronicus III Palaeologos, whose son John was but nine years of age at the time, John Cantacuzenus (c. 1292–1383) was challenged by Andronicus' widow Anna of Savoy and her powerful allies, among whom was the patriarch John XIV Calecas, whose election Cantacuzenus had supported several years earlier. Despite the fact that John had pledged to remain as regent and guardian to the young heir until he came of age, a disastrous and vicious civil war broke out, one of the most eminent victims of which was John's mother, the Lady Cantacuzene. In response, "the Reluctant Emperor," as John was known, proclaimed himself emperor, and successfully put down the attempted coup. In 1354, he abdicated, became a monk, and wrote history. The reference to John Lascaris in the first of these two poems raises the issue, ironically in this context, of a series of events after the death in 1258 of the seven year old boy's father, the emperor Theodore II Lascaris, that resulted in the end of one family's

rule in Constantinople, from 1204 to 1261, through its gradual conniving and finally brutal seizure by the usurper Michael Paleologos, thus beginning the long dynasty of the family to which the young John belonged and John Cantacuzenus demonstrated his loyalty. Nicephoros Gregoras (c. 1292–c. 1360) who is mentioned at the end of the second of these poems, a contemporary of John Cantazuzenus who also served the Paleologue imperial family, wrote a thirty-seven volume *Byzantine History*, which Cavafy used as a source for this poem and a number of others that deal with this historical period.

'Epitaph of a Samian' (p.32)
The poet Kleonymos named in the epigraph as the maker of this sonnet is an invention of Cavafy's. The reference to his patron would date him as "living" between 215 and 163 B.C.

'The Emperor Conon' (p.34)
When the Byzantine emperor Leo III (c. 680–741) announced that he intended to initiate the policy of iconoclasm, the Patriarch Germanus I strongly opposed it, though he believed it wouldn't happen until the reign of an emperor named Conon. Then Leo apprised him of his baptismal name—Conon.

'Hunc Deorum Templa' (p.35)
According to Cavafy's sources, in the year 356, a youthful Julian, who had been raised to the rank of "caesar" and assigned to duty engaging Germanic tribes along the Rhine by his cousin the Emperor Constantius, visited the city of Vienne on the Rhône, where his impressive entrance received a warm and enthusiastic welcome, including the ambiguous one from a blind, old woman recorded in this poem. Temples of the gods and other Roman ruins still stand in lovely Vienne.

'Tigranokerta' (p.38)
The golden city of the ancient kingdom of Armenia, Tigranokerta was founded in the first century B.C. by King Tigranes the Great. Under his expansionist and ostentatious rule, it became famous as a great commercial and cultural center, if only for a brief time. As the speaker of the poem predicts, the Romans did destroy Tigranokerta, as narrated by one of Cavafy's favorite authors, Plutarch, in his *Life of Lucullus*, who conquered and sacked the city in 69 B.C. Ironically, the speaker may not have "split" in time and wound up serving in a celebratory troupe to the victory of Lucullus, who arranged a program in his honor when he learned about the availability of a fine company after their theater, like much of the city, had burned to the ground.

'Nothing About the Lacedaimonians' (p.40)
On September 10, 1931, Cavafy published one of his best-known historical

poems, 'In the Year 200 B.C.,' a work he probably first wrote as early as 1916. Its title sets the poem's point of view 130 years after Alexander the Great's Persian triumphs and just a few years before the Roman conquest of the "new and great Hellenic world" mentioned later in the poem. Lacedaimonians, another name for Spartans, appears in the poem's first line, which is a partial quote from the dedicatory inscription Alexander sent to Athens with the plunder from his victories in Persia as a rebuke to Sparta, which did not participate in his campaigns. 'Nothing About the Lacedaimonians,' the drafts of which are dated July, 1930, should be read along with 'In the Year 200 B.C.' for the additional ironic twist it brings to the levels of address and perspective in play in the published poem.

'Zenobia' (p.41-42)
Septimia Zenobia (Bat-Zabbai in Aramaic; al-Zabba in Arabic), who was born around 240 A.D. and died some time after 274, the "warrior queen" of the Roman colony of Palmyra (in present day Syria), was the second wife of King Septimus Odaenathus and succeeded him after his assassination in 267. Unusually ambitious, beautiful, courageous, and highly cultured (the rhetorician and critic Longinus lived in her court), and expert in creative biographic enhancements, she proclaimed herself "Augusta" and ruled from 268 to 272, conquering several Roman provinces, including Egypt and Anatolia, before she was subjugated by the emperor Aurelius (270–275). There are numerous accounts of what happened to her after her military losses, but the most accepted one is that Aurelius proved merciful and granted her a good Roman life in exile after she was displayed in golden chains (a star even in defeat?) at his triumph.

That Professor Lavagnini's reconstruction of 'Zenobia' abruptly stops in the midst of its ninth line with two crosses, each of which, according to her editorial apparatus, represents two illegible letters, after the word "Macedonia" in Cavafy's single sheet manuscript should come as no surprise considering the great vacillation with which this sole, somewhat inchoate, draft was written. After composing the above brief note on Zenobia, my usual practice for all of the historical figures mentioned in Cavafy's Unfinished Poems, I proceeded to work towards a rendition of the customary "finished" version that has been the goal of every poem in this work. Then I suddenly understood that my commitment to Cavafy to "finish" every one of these poems meant in this anomalous case that I had to "complete" that fragmentary version, which I did unhesitatingly, with the moderate addition of two and a half italicized lines that proceeds syntactically out of his text into an alluring ironic closing informed by several details from some of his favorite sources that I hope is worthy of the splendid Alexandrian.

'Foursome' (p. 43)
This poem (provisionally entitled 'A Company of Four' by Cavafy) and 'Crime' (p. 36) stand out among the 'Unfinished Poems' but also among all

the other poems—published, unpublished and rejected—because of the poet's sympathetic treatment of their attractive young criminals. Many of Cavafy's poems explore the lives of poor young men, an interest he expressed in a note he wrote on June 29, 1908: "I am pleased and moved by the beauty of the masses, of poor young men. Servants, workers, petty clerks and shop attendants. It is the compensation, one imagines, for their deprivations" (*Selected Prose Works*, translated and edited by Peter Jeffreys, Ann Arbor, 2010, p. 136). Although these poems skirt the shadows of questionable life-styles and occasionally suggest illicit or criminal activity, none so openly represent, or celebrate as in 'Crime' and 'Foursome,' beautiful young mobsters. If in finishing them, I have resorted to idiomatic expressions unmistakably rooted in our own underworld culture, I have done so in response to the emotional force that pervades and impels these two extraordinary poems. The unique demand of 'Zenobia' that I *complete* rather than *finish* it, was anticipated by a minor distraction in Professor Lavagnini's reconstruction of 'Foursome' in which the tenth line lacks its second half, a defect Cavafy does not allow in the numerous poems in which he uses this unusual personal form of verse consisting of lines divided by caesura-like spaces into two metrically analogous parts. I have addressed this puzzling omission by shifting the phrase in the first half of the line to the second half and starting the line with the phrase "to Cairo in the winter" on the strength of Cavafy's addition of it in one of the draft stages in the poem's file. Further support for the addition of this phrase comes in the final paragraph of her commentary on the poem: "The trip to Cairo (added here at sheet 4, line 8) symbolizes an easy-going and carefree life," and continues with an account of how Cavafy recalled that his father made frequent trips to Cairo (p. 288).

'Agelaos' (p.44)
Set in Naupactus, a city on the northern shore at the western end of the Gulf of Corinth, in 217 B.C., the site of a peace conference agreed to by the Macedonian ruler Philip V (238–179 B.C.) and the Aetolian League who had been at war with each other, this poem begins with an account of the famous speech given there by Agelaos, one of the Aetolian delegates. The urgency of Agelaos' message, that the Greeks stop fighting each other and pay attention to the impending danger from the winner of the great war to the west of them between Carthage and Rome (the Second Punic War, 218–202 B.C.), succeeded in bringing about a peaceful end to their hostilities. But only temporarily, for, as the poem continues, Agelaos' words were not heeded and "the clouds which are gathering in the west," as he so eloquently and forebodingly put it, did indeed "settle upon Greece." The battles of Cynocephalae (197), Magnesia (190), and Pydna (168), to which Cavafy referred in numerous of his published poems, played decisive roles in the inevitable shift in power over the Mediterranean and Middle Eastern world from Greece to Rome. Cavafy consulted two historical sources, one contemporary and the other ancient, as was his common practice, an article by W. W. Tarn in *The Cambridge Ancient History*, Vol. VII, 1928, and

The Rise of the Roman Empire by Polybius (c. 200–c. 118 B.C.). Agelaos' speech, which is quoted in full in Book V of Polybius' work, is believed to have come from an authentic verbatim version to which the Greek historian had access.

'Diverse Sketches' (pp.45-47)
By designating these four items in the first appendix to her edition of Cavafy's *Unfinished Poems* as "sketches," Professor Lavagnini correctly guides our approach to them as pieces of writing that survive, though hardly in uniform conditions of development, in less advanced states of realization than the drafts collected by the poet in the thirty separate dossiers on which she based her reconstructions of the preceding unfinished poems. Indeed, choosing to label them as "sketches" (*schediásmata*) rather than as "fragments" (*apospásmata*), as others have, lends further support to her definition of them, for the latter term could be misleading inasmuch as it is customary to regard literary fragments as remains of what had once been finished works. In fact, the nearest thing to looking like a fragment in the entire edition, though not in this sense, is the unfinished poem 'Zenobia,' which reflects the poet's decision to abandon or temporarily set it aside rather than the accidental effects of time and nature. And it actually does read more like a sketch, an impression supported by the sole annotation on the single sheet draft of 'Zenobia' in which Lavagnini refers to its composition as a "sketch" characterized by indecisiveness and a fragmentary progress. But it still belongs definitively with the Unfinished Poems rather than with the sketches by virtue of the poet's deliberate classification of it with the other twenty-nine dossiers, each with a title and a date. Though the four texts I have chosen to call 'Diverse Sketches' lack the fundamental groundings of specific titles and dates, which may explain why she calls them "Scattered" (*skórpia*) in her heading, Professor Lavagnini nevertheless suggests titles and speculates about dates for them in the interest of her editorial mission to reconstruct all of Cavafy's "unfinished" compositions.

The inscription in the final line of the first sketch, identifying the emperor as Septimius Severus (145–211 A.D.), provides its temporal setting. The epigraph I have added to the title-less third sketch offers the complete source of the literary allusion in lines 17-18. There is something especially appropriate about the fourth and final sketch being about Julian the Apostate, for it is arguably the last in line, not in terms of chronology but of availability, of Cavafy's extended opus. Julian died in 363 A.D. The first year in the reign of Theodosius I (c. 346–395) was 379. In 362, Julian issued a scornful edict, eventually revoked by Theodosius, forbidding Christian scholars from teaching ancient Greek writers like Homer and Hesiod, whom they had accused of impiety, and urging them to stick to the Matthew and Luke of their Galilean churches. Libanius (314–c. 393), the bad tempered but well-known Syrian pro-Julian sophist who quoted this edict in his book, which the fictional young Alexandrian was reading, is also mentioned by Cavafy in his 1917 poem 'Symeon.'

Dates of Cavafy's Unfinished Poems

The Newspaper Story	(May, 1918)
It Must Have Been the Drinks	(February, 1919)
And Above All Cynegirus	(July, 1919)
Antiochus the Cyzicene	(March, 1920)
On the Pier	(April, 1920)
Athanasius	(April, 1920)
The Bishop Pegasius	(May, 1920)
After the Swim	(June, 1921)
Birth of a Poem	(February, 1922)
Ptolemy Benefactor (or Malefactor)	(February, 1922)
The Dynasty	(November. 1923)
From the "Off the Record" History	(November, 1923)
Julian's Rescue	(December, 1923)
The Photograph	(August, 1924)
The Seven Saintly Children	(January, 1925)
Around the Colonnaded Groves	(1925)
The Patriarch	(February, 1925)
On Epiphany	(May, 1925)
Epitaph of a Samian	(October 1925)
Prick of Conscience	(October, 1925)
The Emperor Conon	(March, 1926)
Hunc Deorum Templa	(March, 1926)
Crime	(July, 1927)
Of the Sixth or Seventh Century	(December, 1927)
Tigranokerta	(May, 1929)
Being Left	(May, 1930)
Nothing About the Lacedaimonians	(July, 1930)
Zenobia	(September, 1930)
Foursome	(1930?)
Agelaos	(April, 1930)
Diverse Sketches	

Uncollected Poems and Translations

Poems

•

Kassandra's story
begins where it ends,
with the gray blade
of bronze against
her throat.

    [once]

The temple serpents
crept to her sleeping,
flicked their gift
upon her lips, tipping
her tongue.

    [or later]

The temple's god
massaged her tongue
with his own,
then spit, when crossed,
into her mouth.

    [one day]

Men would see
she was made like
the golden one,
and her forethought failed
in their ears.

    [then]

Her cunt became
the prize of victors,
victims to be
of the horrors loosed
from her lips.

•

The blade took hold,
her life sped to the shore
of white margins,
where the glossator's wrist hangs
in the air.

The Amorous Drift of the First Hoplite on the Right Wing

The Battle of Mantinea, 348 B.C.

> *All armies are alike in this: on going into action they get forced out rather on their right wing, and one and the other overlap with this their adversary's left; because fear makes each man do his best to shelter his unarmed side with the shield of the man next him on the right, thinking that the closer the shields are locked together the better will he be protected. The man primarily responsible for this is the first upon the right wing, who is always striving to withdraw from the enemy his unarmed side; and the same apprehension makes the rest follow him.*
> —Thucydides, *The Peloponnesian War*, V. 71

The amorous drift of the first hoplite on the right
wing to protect his unshielded side from the enemy
was solicitous of his survival and contagious to the
hoplite to his left whose amorous edging behind his
neighbor's shield for the sake of his survival and to
the hoplite to his left and to his left was considered
dangerous by the generals at Mantinea where both
armies having caught it moved in circuitous front lines
the Athenian phalanx the more impetuous the Spartan
though anxious to hold synchrony with the battle flutists'
pace yielding at last to the devious swerve for survival
that would be perilous if not calamitous to the generals'
plans had they not provided multifarious maneuvers
analogous to the anomalous overlapping of their left
flanks to insure they would in the end be victorious
despite the amorous drift begun by the first hoplite on
the right wing just before the ferocious sweep into chaos.

Day of Disembarkation

It would be odd to call them Odysseys,
being outward, not homeward, bound,

lives made over by landfalls in strange cities
in spaces of magnitudes beyond magna.

Submission to a cyclopean physician
on an island more foreign than Phaeacia,

though penultimate stop of the passage,
certified the transference of homeland

and relegated Peloponnesos or Crete
to a recessive future in memory's eye,

despite a parenthetical return to bring
a woman away, not come back to her.

The couple married America and planted
a tree that would branch and burgeon into

complexions and tongues not seen or heard before
that momentous day of disembarkation.

The Birth of Stand-Up

—*for Tim Whitmarsh*

For a very long time she sat in silence sick at heart
and neither greeted nor embraced anyone,
without laughing and without eating
wasted away longing for her low-girdled daughter,
until the careful, discerning Iambe made jokes that cheered up the lady,
as she would many times after to ease her passion
making her smile and laugh and to lighten her heart.
        Homeric Hymn to Demeter, vss. 197-204

Start a poem from something I've only heard?
Ovid did from something he'd only read,
nosing around, say, in Callimachus
or another of his many sources,
and so became a grander source himself
of the never changing ever changing
state of things he twirled in a permanent
rendition for us to nose around in.
Call this fervent condition "Black Seeing,"
attempts to light up and out of our dark
holds life's stuff redeemed by sight, sound, and touch.
So last summer in Wellfleet in the woods
nature's call awoke me, and as I padded
half asleep through the hall I heard another
from a wild pack of muses in the night
and I'm nothing if not all ears inside
and out to the out-of-sight in the air
of the coywolves' keen singsongsingalong,
no longer tricksters after translation
into Canis latrans [x] lycaon,
able to kill deer or an Actaeon,
disabled to tell he saw what he saw,
and whose hounds' grieving howls were thereupon
silenced by the work of the semivir's
Chiron's hands, an image of their master

*in his cave. (May Pindar's prayer that that wild,
just mind friendly to men live on live on.)
So they say and so we go on saying
axiologótaton, what's worthy
of being told and thereupon still heard,
many-mused sayings one to another
to another, fused in threaded rhythms
of ribbon plaited through Persephone's
tresses, attuning us to her fated
descents below the light and her returns.
Her mother grieved, though, as if for herself
in silence, they say, seated on a slab
of stone named* Laughless *as she was laughless
sitting on the stone cold slab that can kill
comedians and tragedians till
old Iambe became famous for good
and told her, "Said one breast to the other,"
as she jigged, "you remind me of mother."
Then lifting her waist shawl from its bottom,
showing her all, shouted, "Penis Envy?"
and bump-ground her answer out, "Mommycock!"
Then all the women of Eleusis laughed
and Demeter smiled at last and laughing
drank her drink of barley water with mint,
then turned her* nous *to the Rarian Meadow
and other mysteries to come—they say.*

Débat de l'âme et du corps

See you? No. But I think you could go to gehenna in a hand-basket, sweetless, weightless piece, piece poised to disappear into thin air, nonetheless piece of me, marrow of me, the unmarried of married me, the inviolable invisible of the dregs of my more violating than violated decades, still questing—could you be called—spirit, breathless essence of my non-stop breathing, of breaths caressing limbs and syllables, of filaments finely spun to tap the innermost springs, or my mere barking unmixed with wine or water, pure defeated air, yet neither desperate nor despondent, our hopes and promises of savor and savior being practically epoxied to one another, nonetheless destined to part ways on the day of division, but not without a trace of heavier me to fuel your soft blast-off into the wild blue black wonder, my indelible twin, where I can imagine you confronted with the sum of my following my eyes and heart and the answer as to whether or not a pretty girl is like a heresy.

*

I couldn't be sure my dianoia'd annoy ya' because what you give, deeper and darker than words convey, says no, no saying, in its noiseless noetic, leaving me doubtless as to my doubtful state in the wake of your lilting silence, but no you make yourself known without fear that I would mistake you fauxnemically, that I would think I hear voices, for your silence grips me with my problem of having to hear you whom I do not hear because you do not stick it in my ear but in my heart to a T, and that's why I can and do talk back this way because I have the stomach for it, and the guts, and the coraggio, if you will, against your so-called everlasting entirety, your irreducible transparency that stakes its claim to all that is my innermost as alma irredenta, yours, yours, and sheds the batter my running, stinking colors wrap you in that I could not do without, without offering even to meet me part way, no, you must close in the clear though I would offer to grow old as your twin in grisaille.

*

Yes, grayash under granite is my destiny while you go on souling for soul, for more of yourself, supposedly slip the weight, pull a Harry Houdini (forgive me) supposedly, but suppose part of you remains with me, the suppositious soul that belongs to and dissolves in me, or maybe all of you, which would make me your daimon, your singular fate, and would mean I've done all this on my own, and, just as I thought maybe it was you my mere mind that slumbered with me, you will take that small hop, just a six-foot drop, with me into the abyss, my impotent twin, but then I find myself singing of my beginning and end as you stand by grandly and spurn perishability, your hand, as if you have one, strumming strings of air out of me to play the song you allege is yours, and leave me, the so-called poorer pars pro your toto, to parse this maddening grammar of you and me, as if there were no possibility that the sum I am is all I am, first and last, and not groping for you in a state of perpetual desiderium.

Elegiac

in memoriam—

Paul Blackburn (1926-1971), poet and translator of the troubadours,
Federico Garcia Lorca (1898-1936), and others;
Nicholas Howe (1953-2006), medievalist, essayist, teacher;
Traianos Gagos (1960-2010), classicist, papyrologist, teacher.

Es imposible
callarla

"Te quitamos la esperanza,"
the Francoists told him, making him
dig his own grave. And as he did, did he
think *Don't we all?*
        My hope. How can you take
my hope away, when I always knew
I would never
arrive at Córdoba?
        Lorca dug his own grave,
and as he did, became buried treasure.
Blackburn went up in smoke, a way of digging
his own grave.
        "He perdido la esperanza,"
did he think, but for a moment--don't we all?

But hope is the guitar
that weeps for distant things, gives the wound—
¡Oh guitarra! impossible to silence—
that is forever mortal.

Mortmanteau

Speaking of birth and death
we speak as if we own them—
" On the day of my birth…"
"In the event of my death…"
though we can never remember either
nor fully possess the in-between
—the suddenly streaming in-between—
from which we lay claim to them.
So when I speak of my friend
Nick's death I speak of nothing
other than he is death's Nick now
as are "Tom, Dick, and Harry" forever
locked up in mortality's possessive case

Traianos, Adieu

As farewell biddings grow each day
(until my own day to be bid)
in the plain scheme of life lived out,
offenses to this shape of things
still come, bidding farewells be bid
too soon, too soon.
                      Dear friend,
the ancient poet who binds us,
may well bless us with this bidding,
a due fragment to our fragments:
        ] twice met [

            ] what need be [

] good wine and words [

                ] a lifetime of [

Apotropaic

bloody pure scream
a verse shun
in an early light
entrance—ment

delivers line one
may the last not be
an obscure peep
with heels to sheet

but hum to the dance
that turning turns back
la vida's evanescence
as ever in a word

wherein *No*
becomes *Yes*
and flies on a spit
to undo the eye

and by sensing
the air defy
censors and care
for the breath that

never lets go
never descends
always defends
with undeviant fond

The Irrepressible Residue
at the Bottom of the Pensioner's Heart

He never believed less is more,
but less is less, and the more less
there is the less there is in store,
which he had learned but also guessed.

He'd make the most of what was left,
what he was losing day by day,
something make each day of the gift,
which, notwithstanding, wouldn't stay.

He'd let his residue rise and
fall, possibly soar for what seemed
no more than a microsecond,
like something savored, something dreamed.

He thought go on this way until
the grassy or ashen address,
yet finding the means to fulfill
this nonetheless, nevertheless.

A Five in One Wedding Song

for Charis and John

Since in hands
all ceremonies
begin
     you join yours
having reached so far
beyond the reaches of all others
to the topmost bough's top
                       to pick
                                  each other.

      *

The lake joyous
beneath thunder
            arousing
heaven & earth's meaning.

      *

The first miracle
was for marriage
           (dance
Isaiah, dance
     for the wine
that was water
     and the one
that were two.

      *

Jet songs & satellites
ring the planet
but lovers still

only have eyes
for the same old view.

                *

Hand in hand
you take hold of yourselves
get a handle on a world
that gives peach trees and winds
to blow away their petals.

The Twa Poets in Brooklyn Heights

A lufly May afternoon in the year nineteen hundred and sixty-eight,
a lufly with nary a cloud above, with a sweet breeze upon the street,
our small escort brought the two preeminent poets from Scotland,
Hugh MacDiarmid, whose equally held fierce commitments
to Karl Marx and Scottish nationalism often brewed him a cup o' trouble,
and Norman MacCaig, inseparable from MacDiarmid in friendship,
yet separate in so many ways and degrees as to ignite vivid arguing,
the recently retired headmaster in a woolen suit of heaviest weave,
the diminutive communist in tartan kilt, tweed jacket cut at the waist,
plaid hose below his pipe-stem white leggys, a Balmoral bonnet on his top,
the twa poets we brought, after their splendid readings at LIU
in their glittering English and synthetic Scots, we brought them
to a colleague's apartment in Brooklyn Heights well-stocked with Scotch.
The twa poets were no strangers to us and Brooklyn, nor we to them,
their having been invited two years afore to the university's historic
International Writers Conference, at which they deplaned in a state
of ebulliently moderate drunkenness, which they made good effort
to maintain for the duration of the event and occasionally rose above
in moments of grandly uninhibited self-expression, MacDiarmid
with his *poetry like the barrel of a gun*, MacCaig's subtly aimed for
the long haul towards lucidity, winning every heart within earshot,
while I won theirs talking and toasting the singular achievements
of Gavin Douglas, William Dunbar, and Robert Henryson in detail.
So we brought them that day to Brooklyn Heights,
unaware of their invitation to dine in Suffern, NY,
at the home of NYU Professor M. L. Rosenthal,
commonly known—with his permission— as "Mack" to his friends,
who would have to miss their reading at LIU
but they would be able to arrive for dinner
with him and his wife at their Rockland County home
if they would leave immediately after the reading
following his instructions to get there by seven.
We brought them, unaware of this invitation,
and they came, unaware of the distance to Suffern,

to Brooklyn Heights for their post-reading party,
into which we all plunged with great pleasure.
Well into it, a free-form flyting broke out 'tween the twa poets
over some politico-poetical question or other,
the self-defined born atheist and pacifist MacCaig
defending himself against MacDiarmid's charge
that he was an utterly apolitical creature
with a counter-charge of utter confusion
of native traditions and Marxist doctrines,
to which MacDiarmid archly replied,
"Do you really think so, Mr. MacCaig?"
And MacCaig, for all in the room to hear,
"I do indeed, Mr. Grieve!
Do you all know Hugh MacDiarmid
is not his true name?
Tis' Christopher Murray Grieve,
and it's the Grieve part suits him well,
for that is what he especially does to us."
Suddenly, MacDiarmid stepped out of his flyting character,
"Norman, when were we supposed to be at MacRosenthal's?
You had best give him a ring." And as MacCaig left the room,
MacDiarmid continued unopposed, "Mr. MacCaig is daft,
don't you know, fine political quarrels beyond his ken,
though he writes like an angel about his quarrel with himself."
By now MacCaig, his eyes glaring out of his purple face,
burst into the room, "MacRosenthal is furious!" he announced,
"We were to have been in Soofurn by seven and now it's too late.
He gave you directions he said, something about
taking a soobway train to some other place where
we were to take another train that would bring us to Soofurn.
And now it's too late, and we will miss Mrs. MacRosenthal's wonderful
    dinner.
Ah, MacRosenthal is furious!"
Hugh MacDiarmid took this in without a word
and stepped to the corner where his briefcase lay,
carefully removing a bottle of The Macallan Single Malt Whisky,
which had been intended, perhaps, as a dinner party gift

but was now destined for the poet to pour into everyone's glass with precisely measured liberality, then proposed a solemn toast: "Fook MacRosenthal!"
To which the company raised glasses and voices in unison, "Fook MacRosenthal!"

Narcissus Sestina

Having never read a word of Ovid,
he looked the abyss in its face, "O Void,"
he apostrophized, "who make null and void
all for which we are hopeful and avid,
with powerful verses I will avoid
defeat by you, decree you, Void, voided."

A voice replied from deep within the Void,
"All this claptrap might have been avoided
if only you had been sent to Havid
and taught there to read some words of Ovid
(never say Avid), the semi-ovoid
nosed poet you can't afford to avoid.

For he can show you how to be avid
 to detect me in yourself, be devoid
of all that double-trouble that Ovid
learned the hard way, to self-adorn can void
one in the long run; so become voided,
egg you on to your right end *ab ovoid.*"

"You're proposing an already voided
merge by me, of me with you, for Ovid's
words fully convince me that to avoid
trying to stand and balance an ovoid
on one end will wise me up, so avid's
as avid does to brush you off me, Void."

"You don't get it, and still tap an avoid-
dance around the truth of us," snapped the Void.
"And what's this you say about an ovoid?
That's more to add to the pile of voided
words in your pants. You haven't read Ovid
remotely. Your last chance for an avid

grasp of my place in you's to cry, 'O Void,
I look us in the face and am avid
to declare our quarrel has been voided,'
and fear to know yourself no more, avoid
not the chill of my breath in yours."—"Right, Void,"
he replied, "if my cure's still to read Ovid!"

Coda One

The poet, voided, avid to avoid
the ovoidal cold lord of his deep void,
and read a bit, not a lot of Ovid.

OR

Coda Two

So the poet's avid to read Ovid,
and chant, "O Void, our voice as one may void
what can be voided when not avoided."

Pantoum for C.P. Cavafy and a Translator

A task reserved for some mighty king of art,
for himself to find the most fitting language.
He'd be a poet for future generations,
his work never buried inside libraries.

For himself to find the most fitting language
in another is a task intended for a friend,
for work never buried inside libraries
gains a breath of afterlife from that touch.

To another was this task extended as a friend
who'd set it reaching for its fame and to
gain a breath of afterlife from that touch
as it passes from the once and future poet's lips.

He who set it reaching for its fame and
he who found it in a source of grandeur,
pass joined as once and future poets at the lip,
and together say, "Ionia, you own me, Ionia."

He who found it in a source of grandeur,
he'd be a poet for future generations,
and will always say, "Ionia, you own me, Ionia,"
in the task reserved for some mighty king of art.

Who Wants Ice Cream?

At times it's just a matter of fixation
and barely a performance of gustation.

Then there are the thirsty old friends, if you will,
who'd rather swill a favorite libation.

Most young and old, big and small, we must confess,
are nonetheless subject to its temptation.

Scoop on a cone or soft in a cup invites
many delights and cool sorts of sensation.

Fore-savors of love will come with its flavors,
myriad favors from kiss to fellation.

Its Emperor is ours in every regard
with no holds barred or economization.

The Girl in the Gown

for A.E. Stallings

What I learned at a prom, not in a class,
dancing in the dark, holding what I knew,
it's the girl in the gown gives it its class.

I may have been callow, may have been crass,
but I never forgot, never outgrew
what I learned at that prom, before in class.

True content wears form like filling a glass,
content poured anew or as an old brew,
like the girl in the formal radiates class.

Though long gone's the corsage and the band's brass,
eye will testify, throat do and redo
what I learned at the prom, not in a class.

If asked to teach it you'll never surpass
the best you can do that's mere déjà-vu
of what's learned at a prom for the whole class.

So take it right here and not for a pass,
that's what to pursue, there's nothing in lieu
of learning at a prom, not in a class,
that the girl in the gown gives it its class.

Fuck Your Votive Light

—for the hungry poets

Being worst
makes you first
by slight of tongue,
burnt fingerlings
between shiskaboobs
for a cupsized draw
of warmish milk
into a bull's oil eye,
sunny sonny boy,
yuh yellow liver yuh—
so double lick the convection
of your billowy coraggio
flickering outside and in
about the holy rise on high
light of how you vote
yourself from wish-to-toe-
bone bigly, let alone
everyellow indeciduous
as if ego were a permanent
prancing vatic, votary public,
in lieu of an infrastructure righteous
that does not hold unto any of the afters:
so fuh-fuck your vuh-votive light—
put it out like a man.

Five by Georgios Arkadios

I am occasionally visited by this halftavistic persona who has one foot set in the Hellenistic world and the other in our own. Though he knows he'll never make it into The Greek Anthology, *he can't stop trying.*

Count on "Air Charon," your express carrier,
no matter how or where it happens to happen,
crushed like a bug in your high-speed car-smash,
breathing your last in your bed or under the knife,
it's sure to honor the reservation
it made at your zero birth-hour sentence to life
on the solo one-class one-way flight from wherever
direct, non-stop to Hades forever.

*

If one man's poetry roll becomes another's junk
in a rubbish mound at Oxyrhynchus,
then on to funerary wrappings for another,
with immortal lines asleep on mummy cartonnage,
could it synch us to a new, elating Sappho?
Only if the artifex of fact who fuses paths
with long dead word-eating book worms,
his work not exactly up the same alley
as that of Mary Beard or Gregory Nagy,
can hear the distant giggles of laughter-loving Muses.

*

Lucius Commodus lopped off a head of Herakles
then topped off its trunk with one of himself—
he was centuries ahead with his trunk full of folly,
but never tried to clip a poem and drop it onto a canvas
like the solemnly sly synthetic Cy Twombly.

*

Scylla mangles and, as Aristotle argues,
so do bad performers, like those flute players
who manage to yank their coryphaeus' cloak
as they try to play a number about Scylla's
attempts to snatch Odysseus and crew to her rock.

Long before the theatre's decline in Athens,
Archilochos on Paros likened Pasiphile
to a fig tree, the snatch among the rocks
to many a crow, as she gladly puts out for strangers.
To them, this Scylla's the perfect piece, for all her dangers.

*

VILLHELLENELLE

What Schliemann unearthed for the world to see,
down and down strata to Troy VIIa,
Ottomans pitch as their antiquity.

Pergamum, Ephesus, and Priene,
plus the towns 'neath Hissarlik that display
what Schliemann unearthed for the world to see.

Homer's poem's home, though no wooden horsie,
which they'd build if they could—and make it neigh,
Ottomans pitch as their antiquity.

Parts of "Priam's Prize" sneaked to Germany,
pissing-off Turkey, which then tried to stay
what Schliemann unearthed for the world to see.

It's all been theirs since 1453,
beautiful booty—better not betray
Ottomans' pitch as their antiquity.

Baksheesh from Byzantium, valued debris
that's been claimed and renamed to make it pay,
what Schliemann unearthed for the world to see,
Ottomans pitch as their antiquity.

Montana 1939–

for Robert Kelly

"Do you write it the way you remember it?" he asked me. "Yes," I agreed, "I remember it exactly the way I write it."
    —Yiorgos Chouliaras, *Dictionary of Memories*

By then I had had my last conversations
and backyard games with Bakeek and Badak
bilingual avatars made of pure air—
        my Fourth Avenue North
                not Leda's Dioskouroi—
my mother and sister had heard me shouting at
outside the kitchen window before I came in to lunch.
The boys never came in with me but went back home
into thin air—
   "what is their mother's name" Mama asked me,
and I said "Lala, their mother's name is Lala, and she has many children."

*

At that time, the words "President Roosevelt" filled me with reverence, just as God, his only begotten son Jesus, his all holy mother the Virgin Mary, Saint George, and Saints Constantine and Helen, after whom our small Greek Orthodox church, the only one in the entire state, was named, sustained and comforted me. I remember wondering why there wasn't a special place reserved for him in the church, a small icon lit by votive light, my awareness of the distinction between the spiritual and temporal dimensions of things not quite having begun to dawn on me. But in a few months the realization that not everybody loved President Roosevelt struck when one of my father's partners started talking loudly behind the meat counter about a man named Wendell Wilkie, and intensified when I started school the next fall as I watched with dismayed surprise as some of the girls in my first grade class chanted the would-be usurper's name in oscillating rhythm with their violently pumping little white legs under their gravity contesting swings in the playground of the Roosevelt (I hadn't a clue it was named after the ancestral twenty-sixth president Theodore) School. I began to understand for the first time what I had overheard my parents referring warily to as "i republicani" as a palpable threat.

*

"Πεινaί ο άνθρωπος"
There's a big man here, Mama,
up from the alley. He spoke
with her about work for food
at the backdoor and she said
You don't have to work, I will
fix you something good to eat,
but I'm sorry I cannot
invite you into the house.
Then she told me to open
the card table and a folding
chair in the backyard and brought
out a warm bowl of our last
night's avgolemono soup,
which he ate very slowly
as I watched, then she brought out
a plate of scrambled eggs with
toast and a glass of cold milk,
which he ate and drank slowly
as I watched. Then he was gone.
She came out for her dishes
and flatware and said to me.
Poor man was hungry, Yiorgo.

*

in chiaroscuro basement
he marches, marches in place
the sounds of bursting grapes

crushing the dank air with must of Muscat
my powerful papa marches
through memory's fermentation
he must have been a man of forty-eight
but I drink him still a boy of old country vines

*

Death's first dance slipped through the front door in a dream of a dead man I had passed in his coffin, "a good dancer" my parents had told me, and he came in the dark of night as he had been dressed for his departure to dance one last dance up the walls and across the ceiling of our sun parlor coins jangling in his pockets and I ran to a field of prairie grass where I saw a snake coiled, for I had had the German measles and listened to Hitler ranting on the radio that year in which my parents had thought me ready to hear the "αιωνία του η μνημη," the venerable requiem "may his memory be eternal," intoned for the first time.

*

"I saw Santa Claus' boots
as he went up our chimney"
I told my first grade classmates
one of them informed me
sixty-nine years later
to which I quickly replied
"I was a lying poet then
as I'm a lying poet now"
which she firmly rejected
assuring me that back then
I was "extremely earnest
and so intense I made
believers of the class
and it seemed of Miss Craig too"
O strong arm of synecdoche
and fragment's fertility!

*

It wasn't long before the vacant lots behind sitting or standing me in short pants in my mother's photograph collection filled in with houses that boys named Dickie Bates and Eldon McNichol came out of to play. Yet, those empty lots claim a permanence in these photographs of sitting or standing me in short pants in front of my mother's Kodak camera with relatives or friends, with momentous visitors like Athenagoras, Archbishop of North and South America, soon to be named Archbishop of Constantinople, New Rome, and Ecumenical Patriarch, our backs to Fourth Avenue North with those same lots across the street as the background. Now whenever I look at those photographs they elbow their way ahead of my effort to capture memories of Dickie Bates and Eldon McNichol, all but one of each have floated away out of reach as swiftly as a dropped paper cup or sock down a mountain stream: Dickie standing in his underwear behind their front screen door saying he couldn't come out that day, and Eldon and me sitting on the ground in his backyard while his towering bespectaled father (a meter man for Great Falls Electric or Montana Gas I for some reason recall), ever apprehensive about Eldon's safety, ordering us to be careful. O little Eldon, what was your lot in life? And yours, Dickie Bates? Memory's vacant lots.

*

Around the time Picasso
produced his "Man with a Lamb"
I held the back door open
in a spring nightfall chill
as my father carried
a hogtied paschal lamb
from the bed of his pickup
down the basement stairs
and followed him as he asked
despite mother's cries of dissent
and witnessed the scratchy cutting
of the terrified creature's throat
but couldn't turn to run upstairs
not because of anything
he said because he didn't

but because he expected
that I'd understand and stay

*

When my mother handed me the special soft brown cloth and told me to crawl under the dining room table and dust its ornate pedestal and carved feet and then the four side and two arm chairs of the set, it was a sign of company and many good things to come to our table.

*

My father raised and set me
wobbly into the saddle on an
old paint horse with no name now
and told me "hold on to the horn"
but my mother way before
Ed and Patsy Bruce wrote it
or Waylon and Willie sang it
saw to it that her baby would never
grow up to be a cowboy

*

Before our church, which had been bought during the 1920s from the Congregationalists, was renovated and outfitted with a fully equipped basement space for our "doings," we celebrated special events like Greek Independence Day, March 25 (1821), in the local Elks Club meeting hall. We kids wondered what did the B. P. O. E. we saw on the front door stand for, and I wonder now how many of the adults in our community of approximately thirty families and a couple of dozen bachelors did, too. At some now forgotten point in time I learned the letters stood for "Benevolent and Protective Order of Elks," just as one day I became aware that when we spoke the word "AHEPA" it packed a special message of new world commitment, "American Hellenic Educational Progressive Association." So it was at one of my earliest AHEPA-sponsored observations of March 25 "sto Elks Klop chol," which had been rented to us, I trust, with due elkish benevolence, that I gave my very first poetry recitation. My mother taught me the famous six-line poem that Greece's national poet Dionysios Solomos had written in 1825 in commemoration of the total destruction of the island of Psara and its inhabitants by a force of Turks, Egyptians, and Albanians on May 17, 1824, after it had joined the war of independence. As part of the evening's entertainment by the children's generation of piano, singing, dance, and poetry performances, I rose at the sound of my name walked on stage-frightened shaky legs to the head of the hall and gave my recital.

I Katastrophi Ton Psaron

Ston Psarón tin olómavri ráchi
perpatóntas i Dóksa monáchi
meletá ta lambrá palikária
kai stin kómi stepháni forí
yinaméno ápo líga chortária,
pou íchan míni stin érimi gi.

Several decades later I closed a circle by beginning a poetry reading for a Greek-American organization in suburban Chicago by inviting the audience to join me in reciting this poem, after which I began my program with this translation of it.

The Destruction of Psara
   (1825)
—Dionysios Solomos (1798-1857)

On Psara's scorched and blackened ridge
Glory walks alone
musing on the brave young men
and in her hair she wears a crown
woven from the wisps of grass
that had remained on the wasted land.

*

When I was old enough to read
I peripatetically
glimpsed the first of many lessons
in irony and paradox
walking on First Avenue South
to the Pacific Grocery
on an errand for my father
or to meet him for a ride home
after a movie matinee
passing the RED FEATHER SALOON
its name and stenciled logo
dominating its window front
with this lower right warning note
in cursive script *No Indians Served!*

*

I remember seeing Delmar Ladd, who had been elected Student Body President of Great Falls High, as was I some years later, standing empty-handed in a corner hanging out with the other high school kids in one of the town's most popular establishments, the Greek-owned candy and soft-drink shop known as The Liberty Corner, named for its proximity to the Liberty Theater in the Liberty Building. One morning some time later I read in the Tribune that after graduation and the service, Delmar Ladd became a Pullman porter on the Great Northern and lost his life in an accident as his streamliner pulled out of the station, thrown under the train, you might say, by the way things were.

*

In covers up to my chin
wrapped into the arms of the night
that same train's oracular whistle drifts
from its eastward rush into my ears…

Translations

Archilochos (fl. 648 B.C.)

Rough Trade

from a Cologne Papyrus (second century A.D.)

Gone's the bloom from your soft skin, your furrow's
withered too, the ... of foul old age is taking its toll,
    ] and the sweet loveliness has bolted from your longed for face.
    ] for already many blasts of wintry winds
have assailed you, and many, many times...

(rougher trade)

Now that Mother Nature's done her bit,
rewrapping you in sags and wrinkles,
sprinkling your pussy with salt and pepper,
your elective surgeries finish the job
with that blinkless freeze-dried face.

    (roughest trade)

Once your looks were out-of-sight
but now they ought to be again.

Anacreon (*ca.* 563-478 B.C.)

(quoted by Athenaeus (ca. 170-230 A.D.), *The Deipnosophists*, 12. 533e)

Once he stepped out wearing outlandish wasp-like headgear
with wooden dice in his ears and a flayed slice of oxhide hugging his ribs,
the filthy cover of a worthless old shield—Artemon the fraudster,
who conned a living off bread delivery boys and a stable of whores,
whose neck was often strapped to the whipping stock or to the wheel,
whose back was often lashed with a leather scourge
and his hair and beard pulled and plucked.
But now he rides in a chariot wearing gold earrings with accessories
and holds an ivory parasol just like a woman.

Sappho (*fl.* 600 B.C.)

In 2004 at the University of Cologne, three poems by Sappho were found in a papyrus roll that had been recycled as mummy cartonnage. Copied about three hundred years after their original composition, one from among this group of poems provides us with another instance of that great rarity, a finished lyric by this poet. The following translation is from the text of this "newest" of Sappho's poems, as restored by Martin West and published in *The Times Literary Supplement* (June 24, 2005).

It is for you, those lovely gifts in the Muses' violet-scented laps, my girls,
to pursue in earnest, and the keen, vibrant lyre as well:
but my own skin and flesh, once so pliant, old age now
takes over, and my dark hair is turning white;
so my soul grows heavy, and my knees can't hold me,
that once matched the light-footed dance of fawns.
Which things I keep lamenting, but what can one do?
Impossible not to grow old, being only human.
Didn't rosy-armed Dawn, pining with love,
bear Tithonus away once to the end of the world?
Young and handsome then he was, but hoary old age
in time possessed him, though wedded to a deathless wife.

'The Brothers Poem'

A recently discovered fragment in a third century A.D. papyrus
in a private collection, edited and published by Dirk Obbink in
The Times Literary Supplement (February 5, 2014).

[…………..]
Ah, there you go again about Charaxos making landfall
in a well-stocked vessel. Such stuff, I suppose, Zeus
knows all about together with the other gods, stuff you shouldn't even
       contemplate.

Rather have me go and call out
numerous entreaties to Queen Hera
that he get back home here safely navigating
his ship, Charaxos,

and find us safe and sound. As for everything else,
let's just turn that over to the gods.
For good weather can follow foul,
quickly from stormy to serene.

To those whom Olympos' King chooses
to assign a guardian daimon, deliverance from grief
and from that time forth blessed serenity
and great wealth.

As for us, if Larichos would straighten up
and once and for all attain manhood,
from this heavy-heartedness of ours
we'll quickly find release.

C. P. Cavafy

Second Odyssey

A second and great Odyssey as well,
maybe even bigger than the first, but alas,
with no Homer, no hexameters.

Small was his ancestral home,
small was his native hometown,
his entire Ithaca was small.

Telemachos' affection, Penelope's
fidelity, his father's longevity,
his band of old friends, his people's
loyal devotion, the blissful repose of home
poured like rays of joy into the seafarer's heart.

    And just like rays, dissolved.

   A thirst
awoke inside him for the sea.
He hated the air over dry land.
Phantoms out of the West
troubled his sleep every night.
Nostalgia possessed him
for voyages and early morning
arrivals into harbors that
one joyfully enters for the first time.

That Telemachos' affection, that Penelope's
fidelity, his father's longevity,
that band of old friends, his people's
loyal devotion, the peace and repose of home—
Boring!
   —And he was gone.

As the coastline of Ithaca
gradually disappeared from sight
and he set full sail for the way west,
for Iberia, for the Pillars of Hercules—
leaving behind all the Achaean seas—
he felt alive again, felt
liberated from the oppressive ties
to familiar and domestic matters.
And his adventurous heart exulted
in cold blood, with nary a drop for love.

(This poem, never published in Cavafy's lifetime, was written in 1894, the same year he wrote an essay in Greek, also unpublished before the poet's death, entitled "The Last Days of Odysseus," which explores the treatments of the epic hero by Dante in Canto 26 of the *Inferno* and Tennyson in his poem 'Ulysses.'" See Cavafy, *Selected Prose Works*, translated and annotated by Peter Jeffreys, University of Michigan Press, 2010, pp. 105-111.)

The End of Antony

But when he heard the women crying
and lamenting his sad plight,
madam with her asiatic gestures,
and the slaves with their barbarized Greek,
the pride in his soul stood up,
his Italian blood turned sick,
and those things he'd blindly idolized till then
seemed strange and indifferent—
his fiery Alexandrian life—
and he said, "Don't cry for him, it's not becoming.
Better they should praise him
for proving to be such a great ruler,
and for acquiring such wealth and possessions.
And now if he's down, he hasn't gone down basely,
but as a Roman by a Roman vanquished."

(1907)

*(This translation—once for, and now in memory of,
my Roman friend Luigi Attardi, pen name Nail Chiodo.)*

And I Leaned and Lay on Their Beds

When I entered that house of pleasure,
I didn't remain in the chambers where they keep,
with a certain propriety, to recognized ways of love.

I entered the hidden rooms
and leaned and lay on their beds.

I entered the hidden rooms
believed shameful even to name.
But not shameful to me—for then
what kind of poet or artist would I be?
Better to abstain. That would be in greater accord,
much greater accord with my poetry,
than for me to take joy in the commonplace rooms.

(1915)

Michalis Katsaros (1920–1998)

Those You See

Those you see you'll come across once more
you'll get to know them once again
one of them called Bill and another Ben

Those you see you'll come across once more
you'll get to know them once again
into this world they will return
and with a greater pride to burn

Those you see you'll come across once more
you'll get to hate them once again
but one you'll not find anymore
the youngest, most bitter, and most dear
the one and lonely, strong and free of fear

Him you'll never see again to hurt
and his great heart to tear apart
him you'll never find again the one who's guarded by the stars
the one guarded by his sun, guarded by the moon

He who has the gift, the youngest
the most bitter and most dear
for him I alone await, I alone am here

(From the Greek "Aftous pou vlepis,"
this translation is for Vassilis Lambropoulos.)

Luis Cortest

The Subway Station

(from the Spanish *"Estación del metro," 1983*)

Today, agitated and scared
I waited three hours for you for nothing.
I came looking for one more look
And to say goodbye
My fingers shivering with cold fear
My hot hands sweating with worry.

I came looking but didn't find you.
I wanted to say it was all my fault
That none of it was your fault.
I wanted to look in your eyes to feel
What I'd felt last night
And to burn your face in my memory.

But it never happened.
I waited three hours for you for nothing.
You gave me no chance
To let loose my sorrows
Nor start to forget you.

www.ingramcontent.com/pod-product-compliance
Lightning Source LLC
Chambersburg PA
CBHW031207160426
43193CB00008B/542